IMAGES
of England

ISLINGTON
THE SECOND SELECTION

The original Angel inn of antiquity was pulled down in 1819. This version, seen here at the beginning of the twentieth century was to become a Lyons teashop in 1923 – part of a large chain. Here, the horsebus is advertising an appearance by the famous escapologist Harry Houdini at the Hippodrome. No doubt many middle class Islingtonians would be visiting the show, but more than fifty per cent of the population at the time would not have been able to afford such West End luxuries, having to find their entertainment locally at a modest cost.

IMAGES
of England

ISLINGTON
THE SECOND SELECTION

Compiled by
Gavin Smith

TEMPUS

First published 2002
Copyright © Gavin Smith, 2002

Tempus Publishing Limited
The Mill, Brimscombe Port,
Stroud, Gloucestershire, GL5 2QG

ISBN 0 7524 2461 0

Typesetting and origination by
Tempus Publishing Limited
Printed in Great Britain by
Midway Colour Print, Wiltshire

Contents

ISLINGTON. St. Mary's Church.

The steeple of St Mary's church rides high above the surrounding buildings in 1906. The church, a rebuild of 1754 to the design of Laurence Dowbiggin, had replaced a venerable medieval structure which was actually blown up by explosives to the great excitement – not to say trepidation – of the local inhabitants, to make way for the new building. This certainly looked as good as many a city church and its elegance marked the transition from village to fashionable suburb though fields for a time still separated the district from London proper.

Introduction

The speed at which London's suburbs grew still seems miraculous looking back over two centuries. Studying the first half of the nineteenth century, valuable clues reveal Islington's transformation at a time when the process was beginning to gather pace. A quote from a *Penny Magazine* supplement of 1840 shows the contradictions between the rural nature of a burgeoning agricultural business, and the growing size of the operation due to the rise in local population which was increasing the demands on food supplies:

'A day at a London dairy is a very early day. It begins when nearly all the world is fast asleep and ends when the fashionable world has not long risen. It is a day which reminds us of the "good old times" of Queen Bess, when a breakfast of beef and ale was taken at five or six o'clock in the morning and when a large portion of the day's labour was completed before noon. We do not in this mention of dairies allude to the shops or shop-kitchens of the humble dealers by whom a large proportion of the London families are supplied with their daily pennyworths of milk... but to the establishments of those large proprietors of milch cows, by whom the retail dealers are in many cases supplied. It is not improbable that many persons living in the heart of the metropolis and who scarcely see a cow from year's end to year's end, may be ignorant of the existence of such places; entertaining the opinion that

Laycock's Dairy – Milking Shed.

each retail dealer draws "his new milk from the cow" in his own shed a few hours before the world's breakfast time. Many do so, no doubt; but there are also many who cannot boast of possessing a cow and whose dairy proceedings consist in buying milk to sell again at a profit in small quantities. Let us see if a pleasant day may not be spent in studying the commercial machinery by which large towns are supplied with milk. We shall have to rouse the reader from his bed at two o'clock in the morning, and beg of him to accompany us to Islington, a very land of cows, from which more parts of London are supplied with milk than is generally imagined. Proceeding northward from the well known "Angel", we come to a division of roads at Islington Green... following the western branch known as Upper Islington we pass Islington church; and a little before we arrive at Highbury, an inscription on a gateway at the left points out to us "Laycock's Dairy and Cattle Layers". Through this gateway (supposing the permission of the proprietor to have been obtained) we enter, and soon find ourselves surrounded by buildings spread over a vast extent of ground and consisting principally of sheds, barns and granaries... we will direct our notice to a large range of cow or milking sheds on the right hand side.

As three o'clock approached, a scene of bustle presents itself. Milkmaids, whose scarcely intelligible language indicates Wales to be their native country and whose ruddy faces give evidence to the healthiness of their employment, arrive at the dairy, bring their pulls and stools to the milking sheds and make preparations for milking the cows... each of these milkmaids has a handkerchief bound round her head... each one places her wooden pail – so neat and white and clean, that one almost doubts it ever could be dirty – beneath the cows, sits on her stool, rests her head against the side of the animal and milks until the pail be full or until the cow has yielded her mornings supply. The cows being ranged in tolerably regular order and a considerable number being milked at one time, the whole presents a scene, by no means picturesque. The number of milkmaids bears some convenient proportion to the number of cows; so that all the latter, four or five hundred in number, may be milked in the course of about an hour or an hour and a half. Each milkmaid draws the milk from several cows; but the mode of proceeding is the same in all; the animal is fastened to the stall, and remains quiet during the process of milking.

Of the very large quantity of milk which is thus obtained within this time, by far the larger proportion leaves the dairy immediately. In some instances, women provided with a wooden yoke, carry away the milk in pails, while in other instances the milk is put into tall metallic vessels and carried away in carts. The persons to whom the milk is thus sent are retail dealers who purchase their milk at these large establishments and retail it at a profit which affords them the means of subsistence...'.

What echoes these descriptions ring out for us. The organization of milk supply in 1841 was already the foundation of what might be called today an 'agri-business'. Yet some of the distribution, presumably to local houses in the village of Islington and a few terraces lining the highways was still in the hands of milkmaids. Islington was not yet included in London but was an important supplier to that city. Supplements to weekly magazines were already being read and directed at the middle classes of the suburban villages like Islington – which meant that thirty years before the 1870 Education Act promoted education for the masses, sufficient numbers of population had been to school and provided a readership for popular magazines. Soon after this, the tide of bricks and mortar would flow over the fields, followed by the corner shops and dairies, many of them run by migrants from Welsh farming depressions. These dairy shops (Jones the Milk, Evans the Dairy) would continue in existence up to the 1960s and '70s.

Gavin Smith
October 2001

A Victorian Account of the Traces of Early Man in Highbury

The following extract from John Evans's *Ancient Stone Implements of Great Britain* (1872), pp. 524-5, charmingly records the discovery of an Early Stone Age flint tool in what was then a brick pit in the fields of Highbury New Park before the construction of further housing. Not far away in other fields, the harvest was being gathered.

'The fluviatile beds in question are exposed in two brick-pits at Highbury New Park, near Stoke Newington, and attention was first called to them in August, 1868, by Mr. Alfred Tylor, F.G.S.

On reading the account of this discovery, I was at once impressed with the possibility of the occurrence of Palæolithic implements in this deposit; and accordingly in September, 1868, I visited the pit with the view of searching for them, taking with me my youngest son, Norman, who has a quick eye. [...] Our search was soon rewarded, for immediately on descending into the lower part of the pit, where the shell-bearing beds were exposed, my son picked up the remarkably well-formed implement shown [below]. It was not *in situ*, but was lying in the bottom of the pit; and judging from the staining upon a portion of its surface, it appears to have been derived from brick-earth, rather than from the more shelly beds below.

It is well adapted for being held in the hand as a sort of knife or chopper, having a thick rounded back formed of the natural crust of the nodule of flint from which it was made. [...] No other specimens have as yet been found at Highbury.'

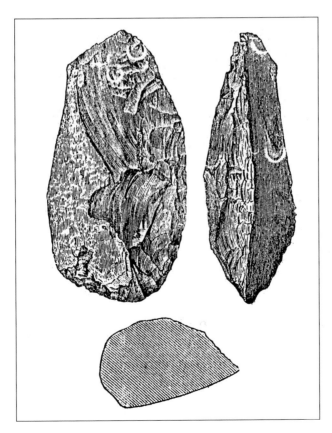

At the beginning of the nineteenth century, St Mary's steeple presided over a rather sleepy huddle of buildings, some of wooden construction and with pantile roofs, dating from different centuries. Even so, there are signs of local industry and commerce with a premises in the foreground offering to renovate gentleman's hats of the period (1808).

One
Romance of a
Bygone Age

From a past rich in country village delights comes this view of a cricket match at the White Conduit House. The landlord of this pleasure resort for Londoners in the 1740s had converted it from a simple beerhouse, by adding a storey and building a 'long room' onto the original. This stood near a water supply (conduit) marked by a stone, which had up until 1654, supplied the London Charterhouse. This same Robert Bartholomew provided bats and balls for games of cricket. In 1786, Thomas Lord looked after the pitch. By the next year he had been poached by the predecessor of the present Lords cricket ground and it is his name which graces the home of English cricket. Thus, it all began in Islington. The resort saw many famous visitors. Oliver Goldsmith the famous writer used to take tea with his friends here often after earlier dining at Highbury Barn. He mentions in particular the White Conduit House for its 'hot rolls and butter' in his book *Citizens of the World*. The friends had thus spent the whole day breathing in the wholesome Islington country air.

Remains of the Roman camp at Barnsbury. This was one of two eminence's on which camps were discovered, the other being at Highbury. At Barnsbury the most was clearly visible in what later became Barnsbury Square. This was finally drained and made up in 1825. A small part of the entrenchment remained in the garden behind Montfort House.

Canonbury Tower at the beginning of housing development. The house and tower was a Manorial possession of the Priory of St Bartholomew, Smithfield Prior William Bolton (1509-32) either built or reconstructed a house on the site. His rebus or punning symbol (a bolt in a tun –or barrel) survives, built into a house in Alwyne Place nearby. (The author's previous volume on Islington in this series describes this.)

The old Tudor house on Newington Green, *c.* 1811. There were two houses on the Green that appeared to have once been grand mansions. This one at the north-west was, by this time, converted into several tenements. There was a tradition among the local inhabitants that the house had once been a seraglio or house of concubines to which Henry VIII came. A second house on the south of the Green also like this, bore signs of carved figures and gilt wall paintings of great richness. The area around was certainly the haunt of nobility such as the Dudley family, and there is a letter by the Earl of Northumberland probably written from this house.

The galleried yard of the Angel inn, in its great coaching days at the end of the eighteenth century.

A south-east view of Copenhagen House in 1783. Another country scene which later became the site of the clock tower of the Caledonian cattle market. The Great Northern Railway also built its 'Copenhagen Tunnel' underneath the hill to carry its trains northwards from Kings Cross. It is said to have been opened by a Dane during James the

First's reign for the use of Danish nationals living here. The earliest record of it as a pleasure resort is in 1762, but it was probably operating in the seventeenth century. In the 1780s one of the earliest 'Fives-Courts' in London was established. John Cavanagh – a very famous champion – used it.

The old Queen's Head, Islington. Demolished in 1829, it was described as one of the most perfect illustrations of ancient domestic architecture in the vicinity of London. The names of several Elizabethans, including Sir Walter Raleigh, are associated with the inn which stood at the corner of Queen's Head Lane in Lower Street (later Essex Road).

Another of the ancient inns of the village 'The Crown' is recorded in this print. It was superseded before 1811 by the 'City Farm House'. It appeared to have once been the home of the member of the Mercer's Company, containing an old stained glass window with their arms.

16

The Pied Bull once stood behind Frederick Place and was an Elizabethan hostelry, where Sir Walter Raleigh is alleged to have stayed – he is variously said to have smoked the first tobacco in England at this inn and at the Old Queen's Head. When it was pulled down in 1830, the parlour window contained stained glass with the arms of Sir John Miller of Islington and Devon.

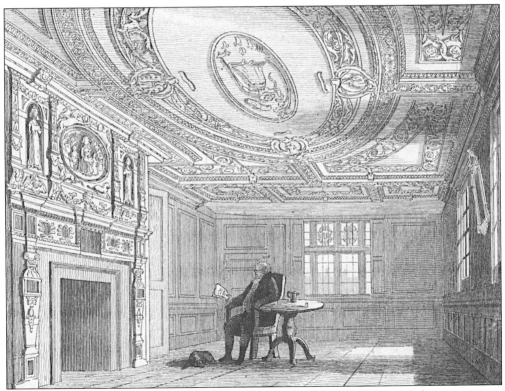

The amazingly richly carved interior of the Pied Bull recorded in 1819 for an Ackermann print.

Bird's eye view over part of Islington, showing the houses and fields towards London, 1819. Islington church and St Paul's can be seen and the fashionable terraces beyond the fields advancing year by year.

Naive print of 'Busby's Folly', a pleasure resort in 1731. It consisted of tea gardens and bowling green and existed as early as 1664, getting its name from Christopher Busby or Busbee, who kept the 'White Lyon'. By the 1760s it was 'Penny's Folly', Islington New Road (Pentonville Hill). The Belvedere Tavern and Tea Gardens were built on the site around 1780.

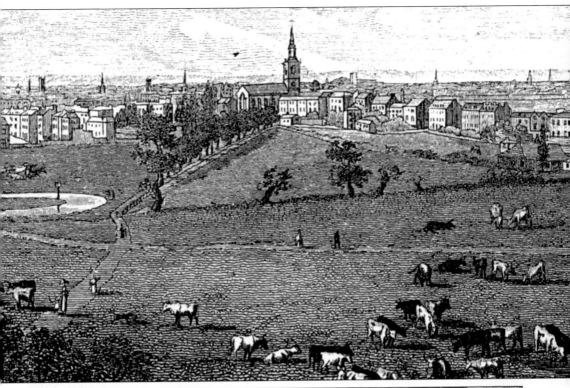

The Rosemary Branch Tea Garden in 1846, a well known pleasure resort from 1783. The audience watches from the arcade surrounding the performance arena – the premises covering three acres. Pony racing is taking place on the circuit, while in the middle, tight rope dancers perform on the high and low ropes. These were favourite entertainments, with performing horses and balloon ascents.

The Birmingham 'Tally-Ho' coach passing the Crown at Holloway in 1828. This was an important highway for coaches going northwards.

On the bank, Highgate West Hill – a London to York coach struggles with the incline, 1810.

Faden's map showing the southern part of Islington in 1822. At the top are Mr. Laycock's cattle sheds. North of the unfinished Duncan Terrace is Mr Rhodes' Cow Lair. The Watch House stands at the point of Islington Green. The New North Road extension to Highbury Corner is awaiting construction across the brickfields and mineral springs of Canonbury fields, and there is a riding school nearby.

The fields to the south... fashionable strollers pass through the country walks by Sadlers Wells and the New River Head in 1730. New Tunbridge Wells in the middle, where the nobility and others came to taste the spa waters, had at first been called Islington Wells and Islington Spa,

Sadlers Wells race course – one of many attractions offered in 1806. The Chalybeate Well was discovered by one Sadler, who had opened a music hall here as early as 1683. Claiming it had been a medieval holy well enabled Sadler to charge 3d a head to patronise its curative properties. John Evelyn, the diarist, was one of hundreds who flocked to its waters until the rival New Tunbridge outbid its claims.

until it was realised that the similarity in taste and medicinal value to the water at the Kentish spa required a second renaming. In 1733 it was so renowned that the daughters of King George II, Princess Amelia and Princess Caroline paid a visit.

The artificial watercourse constructed by Sir Hugh Myddleton to bring water to London in the reign of James I, had settled down into a tree fringed stream of much beauty at many points in its route, such as here at Willow Walk.

An elegant view of the meeting of the Upper and Lower Roads at Islington Green, with horse drawn coaches coming out of both. Note the Watch House at the point of the Green, and the tall hats of the men in the picture, Regency style.

Looking along 'Upper Islington' of the early nineteenth century. Fashionable shops and dresses abound, with the occasional street lamp to improve visibility after dark.

An 1830s scene in Upper Holloway with a small flock of sheep being driven along the middle of the road in imminent peril of being run down by a fast coach from the north.

Highbury Barn is developing from a country lane into a desirable suburb in the 1830s. The only drawback might be the noise from the pleasure gardens with their 'Leviathan' dancing platform and excited patrons at night.

The Angel inn corner in 1818. Two long distance coaches are visible. Despite this, a mixed group of sheep and cattle are being herded down the middle of the High Street, presumably towards Smithfield.

A view from Maiden Lane (now York Way) of the Regent's Canal in the 1830s, shows how the fields of south-west Islington have largely given way to urban and industrial activities. The factory in the distance with its two smoking chimneys to the left of Thornhill Bridge on the Chalk (later Caledonian) Road, later retained a link with agriculture becoming Thorley's Cattle Food works in around 1854.

Two

A Populous Parish

Islington Central Library, Holloway Road

The noble frontage of the Islington Central Library on the corner of Fieldway Crescent, c. 1912. The public library network in the borough was established not without fierce opposition in the Edwardian era. The front entrance once opened onto an interesting passageway with doors in and out of the lending library on the left, and a children's department on the right. A classical staircase gave access to the delights of the reference library. Modernization has moved the public entrance to the rear of the building – once the way in and out for the staff. The magic of the old dignified access has somehow been lost, but that is progress.

The Angel crossroads. It is a sign of the rapidity of progress in the twentieth century that this street scene seems to date from an even more distant era than that of just a century ago. Modes of transport, work and leisure and the buildings have all passed through dozens of changes.

In spite of the springing, a ride in this Finsbury Park to Peckham bus must have been a bumpy one. The solid wheels and the bad or cobbled surfaces of London streets at the beginning of the twentieth century ensured this. It was lucky that although they led a hard life, the horses on the front were able, almost instinctively, to anticipate the erratic movement of other vehicles including the earliest motor buses with their poor steering.

NEW ELECTRIC TRAMS AT FINSBURY PARK.

The new electric trams at Finsbury Park in 1904. The new method of transport with its smooth ride soon posed a threat to the railways which then served dozens of local city and suburban stations within short distances of each other.

ESSEX ROAD. N.

Essex Road underground railway station – another new method of getting around town, opened on 4 February 1904. This tube was an offshoot of the Great Northern main line railway and was meant to be a feeder from their network into the city. The tunnels being larger than other tubes were originally intended to accommodate main line rolling stock, but ended up with their own dedicated cars.

Islington.
Town Hall, Upper Street.

The Town Hall when Islington became a Metropolitan Borough, was the original Vestry Hall of the old Parish of St Mary Islington, the nineteenth century building of 1859-60. This stood on the corner of Florence Street. It served the borough until the new Town Hall on the site further west gradually came into service between 1923-1925. The site was then sold and after 1927 became the Lido Cinema.

The interior of the Parish and Borough Church of St Mary's is seen here after renovation and re-opening, 30 April 1904.

Islington Workhouse.

The massive frontage of the Islington Workhouse, still an essential institution of local government in the early twentieth century. The population of the borough in 1901 was 335,238 – a tenfold increase on 1831. This was a larger total than Belfast, Newcastle or Edinburgh.

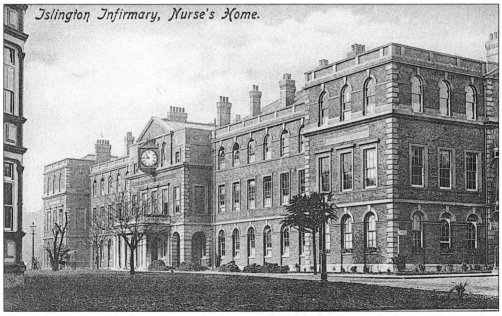

Islington Infirmary, Nurse's Home.

The infirmary attached to the workhouse needed this large nurse's home. The gradual realisation that much poverty was caused by failing abilities and illness caused a large part of the workhouse role to be transferred into infirmary or hospital and medical facilities. These eventually laid the foundation for the National Health Service.

Some of the staff of the Islington Infirmary, their uniforms spotless, all under the eagle eye of matron and her sisters who ruled a tight ship with little waste. The medical superintendent seems embarrassed at being photographed with so many females.

Inside Ward A4, the effort put into cleanliness is immediately obvious. All of the top windows were open to let in God's fresh air, while every member of staff looks alert and ready for emergencies.

The Great Northern Hospital, Holloway Road (later the Royal Northern) was opened on 17 July 1888 by Edward Prince of Wales, the future King. It had been running since 1856 on a smaller scale at York Road and then at Caledonian Road. In 1923, a new casualty department was added which was also the Borough War Memorial, and an archway inside was inscribed with the names of 1,337 Islingtonians killed in the First World War. The exterior with its street scene is pictured in 1912.

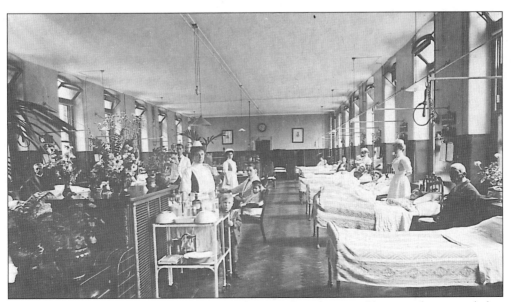

Again in the Great Northern's Victoria Ward we see the tidiness and hygiene that prevailed in hospitals in the days of the all powerful matron and her cohorts of senior nurses, 1912.

The dramatic but murky scene of the *Flying Scotsman* departing from Kings Cross Station. Though a fraction over the border, Kings Cross was very much Islington's main line terminus. In the days of steam, the scene was coloured by various shades of grey – the predominant hue

e 1940s with all its shortages, yet the departure of the Scots expresses brought excitement and a sense mance, as with the official rushing the mail trolley towards platform 10.

The Convent of Our Lady of Sion – a balloon view of the late nineteenth century (above) and a view in the courtyard, *c.* 1910 (below). The Convent with the Church of the Sacred Heart both date from 1870, serving the local Roman Catholic community.

On 15 July 1905, the Duke of Fife, Lord Lieutenant of the County of London officially unveiled a memorial to the memory of the 110 Islingtonians who lost their lives in the South African or Boer War, 1899-1902. The bronze figure of 'Glory' with a wreath held high is probably one of the most artistic memorials in London. This is not surprising as the artist was Sir Bertram McKennal, R.A., KCVO (1863-1931) who also designed the Memorial Tomb of Edward VII at St George's Chapel, Windsor – the 1913 National Memorial to the artist Thomas Gainsborough, and the coinage of George V, among other commissions. The figure of 'Glory' stands at the southern edge of Highbury Fields.

TO THE INHABITANTS OF

St. MARY'S ISLINGTON.

LADIES AND GENTLEMEN,

We the constant **Dustmen** of this district in the employ of Mr. C. STARKEY, do make humble application to you for a **Christmas Box**, which you are usually so kind as to give, and to prevent imposition on you, and fraud on us, (which is frequently attempted by giving BILLS similar to the one now presented) we humbly hope you will not give your bounty to any who cannot produce a MEDAL of the Coronation of King George and Queen Charlotte Sep. 22nd. 1761, .on one side & Britannia on the other.

W. PRESTON, & T. POWELL.

No Connection with the Roadmen.   Please not to return this Bill.

Islingtonians have always been individualists, as witness this circular from the dustmen of the district, finding a unique way to prove their identity in their application for a Christmas Box in the nineteenth century Islington Vestry days.

A plea of another sort, featuring royalty and in the form of the universally used postcard sent out in August 1914.

Holloway Castle E 14399

The original Holloway Prison was modelled on Warwick Castle, constructed between 1848-52 and designed by J. Bunning, who also designed the Metropolitan Cattle Market. In the nineteenth century it was a 'double' prison, housing both men and women, but from 1903 only took women. Oscar Wilde spent his remand time here in April/May 1895 but it is especially remembered as the place where suffragettes were abused.

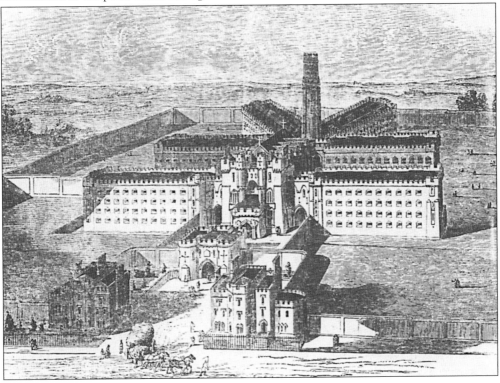

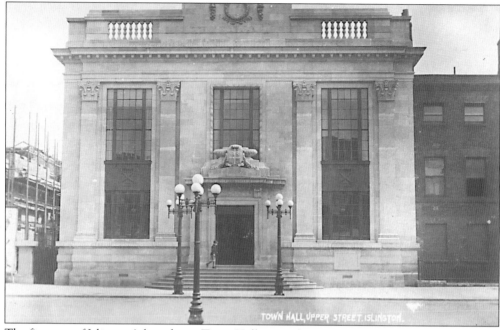

The first part of Islington's brand new Town Hall is seen here with its forecourt and stylish lamp standards. Work is going ahead on a second phase to the left of the image. The extension was to be opened on 10 October 1925 by Councillor Sidney Harper, Mayor from 1922-1925.

Trams and trolleybuses sheltered overnight in Holloway Depot. The 1930s saw the wide ranging replacement of trams by trolleybuses. After the Second World War, trolleybuses were themselves replaced by petrol buses. Thus Holloway Depot had seen three forms of road transport.

Three
Shopping Around

The old houses on Islington High Street by the Turnpike Gate. Many were converted into shops as the 'Angel' became fashionable in Regency days. The Three Hats, on the right, was one of a number of taverns here visited by pleasure seekers on half days and holidays, when the tea gardens and inns made 'Merry Islington' a place of popular resort. In 1767, Mr Sampson displayed 'feats of horsemanship' at a commodious place built for that purpose in a field adjoining the 'Three Hats'. A band was also hired to accompany this entertainment. There were in fact more rival showman trying to outdo each other in horse-riding tricks at different locations around London. Later, the neighbouring buildings acquired shop fronts selling tea, groceries and other items to members of 'Polite Society'.

Cattle Market, Caledonian Road *King's Cross, London. N.*

Although this illustration is labelled the 'Cattle Market, Caledonian Road', the activity which is taking place behind the railings is the General Market which took over on certain days of the week and became an established feature, attracting a very cosmopolitan crowd, turning over second hand goods and antiques.

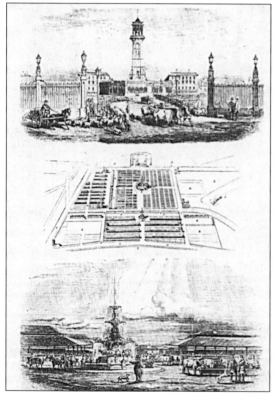

Panorama of the original plan of the New Metropolitan Cattle Market complete with fountain (at bottom).

Trading 'on the stones' was the term used by those who set out their wares on the cobbles. Twice a week it was said that on the stones – 'like Harrods' – you could buy anything that could be bought. Many exciting bargain antiques were discovered here by those with the knowledge to pick them out. Thus the market became known far and wide as a tourist attraction. After the Second World War, the market migrated to South London.

The Chapel Market – scenes from the first ten years of the twentieth century. This was the local people's market and on some days there was such a crowd on the pavements and in the roadway that it might take thirty-five minutes to get from one end to the other.

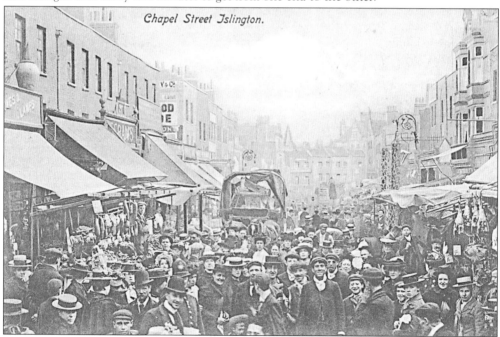

Chapel Street Islington.

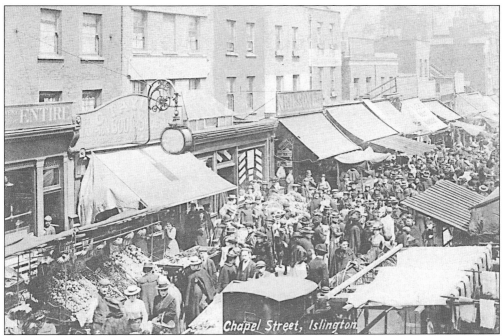

Chapel Street, Islington

The shops along the pavements of Chapel Market are clearly seen in these images of the Edwardian era. There are also a number of public houses – after all it was thirsty work shopping and trading, and sometimes the household budget or the takings from the stall would shrink in the course of a day spent slaking one's thirst now and then. At this time, the shops were mostly local firms but national multiples were increasing their outlets and names such as F. W. Woolworth and Marks and Spencer arrived, often taking over a number of the original premises to accommodate their larger stocks. J. Sainsbury is already in Chapel Market as can be seen in the bottom picture.

Chapel Street Islington N.

The middle section of Caledonian Road between the North London railway bridge and the canal bridge (Thornhill Bridge), was also a lively local shopping area and there were a number of other businesses as well as shops, something of a small industrial location for various manufacturers. Above is Wheeler's the Printers with the slogan 'The Best and Cheapest Printer' who in fact produced this postcard. Below, we see the local style of advertising the shops and businesses on large painted notice boards standing high above the wide pavements, c. 1909.

The inside of the Home and Colonial Stores Upper Street shop in 1905. Still trading up until after the Second World War, they were one of the forgotten multiple grocer rivals of Sainsbury's. Another such was Pearks. The tiled floor down the middle, the different department's service counters for cheese, bacon etc. are all similar to early Sainsbury's and none was without the high cashier's payment cubicle.

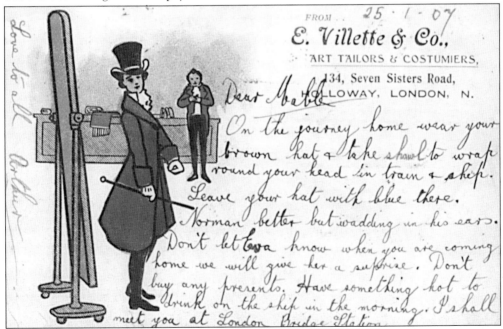

This charming business postcard relates to E. Villette and Co., who are described as 'Art Tailors and Costumiers' suggesting a connection with the stage and fancy dress or ceremonial dress. The postcard was sent to a member of the family from France in January 1907. The family may have hailed from the village of Merbrault in Orne, France to set up the business in England.

A wonderful scene of Islingtonians welcoming Royalty to the Borough at the beginning of the twentieth century, outside the large drapers shop of T.R. Roberts in Upper Street. We do not know the exact event, but it obviously caused great excitement and brought out a large crowd of spectators. Notice the raised causeway, dating back centuries which originally enabled the superior classes to keep their feet free of the muddy morass in the carriageway. It ran from the

Angel to St Mary's church and had by this time been provided with the steps which could still be partly seen along its length. T.R. Roberts had taken over the business of Rackstraw's and the drapery 'emporium' was known for its quality far and wide, employing at one time about 250 people. The store closed in 1953. Note the curious numbering '219½'.

The Nags Head was an important shopping centre even in 1912. As well as shops, it had restaurants and entertainment. The famous Jones Brothers stores (out of picture, right) was one of the well known businesses here and was still going as part of the John Lewis empire until the end of the twentieth century. Its name lives on in the Jonelle range of fabrics.

Peck's of 10-16 Essex Road were a local store which spread itself by moving into adjoining shops over a period of time. There is a tram stop outside.

Southgate Road on the south-east edge of the borough had acquired a terrace of neighbourhood shops and a two horse tram service by this time, 1905.

The Broadway, Highbury Park.

The upward slope of The Broadway, Highbury Park, also has a fine array of local ground floor shops with apartments above. The rider on horseback was perhaps not such a rare sight in 1906. Within seven years, the Arsenal Football Club were to arrive in this area, taking over part of the grounds of St John's Divinity College.

Upper Street, with Rackstraw's famous drapery establishment on the right and the Highbury Furnishing Company on the left, 1912.

Holloway Road, c. 1904, with a plethora of stylish shops, encouraged by the Edwardian commercial boom. A sideways view of the tower and an advertisement for Jones Brothers is opened up on the left hand end.

The Jones Brothers area of Holloway Road in 1920.

The Nag's Head public house on the corner of Seven Sisters Road and the row of shops beyond in 1920. The traffic consists of trams, early motorbuses and vans, a horse carriage of some description and a great number of pedestrians.

A typical café, or dining rooms to use the parlance of the time, situated in Liverpool Road in 1904. The establishment also offered bed and breakfast. Such places were a boon to the large number of young bachelors making their way in the big city during this period.

Four
Putting on a Show

The Drayton Park Bear.

Islington knew many ways of putting on a show. Sadly, the majority of the public in 1908 did not see the cruelty attached to parading a performing bear. It was allowed to tour the streets and show off its tricks – as here in Drayton Park, drawing a crowd of children and adults. Islington also had more civilised forms of entertainment, for instance in the form of theatres and later of course, cinemas. The Agricultural Hall was a great exhibition centre which staged many of the national events. Later these would migrate to Olympia and Earls Court complexes.

The complicated frontage of the Agricultural Hall from Upper Street. The main entrance was originally in Liverpool Road (see Images of England series: *Islington*). The hall is hosting the Confectioners and Bakers Exhibition. To the right, there is a large advertisement for the famous Music Hall star Little Tich, appearing at the Empire.

To the Cattle Show
300 TRAMCARS AN HOUR

THERE are many shows at the Agricultural Hall, Islington, and one of the greatest of these is the Cattle Show—in size and importance the leading fat stock display in the world. It is the farmers' Wembley. Most of the visitors between Monday, the 8th, and Friday, the 12th December, will come from the shires, but there will be much to interest the country-loving Londoner too. Three hundred tramcars an hour— 5 a minute!—stop at the Agricultural Hall itself or at The Angel, close by.

The Services and Fares to the Angel are :—

From				
Aldersgate	...	...13	71	77
Bloomsbury	...	...	51	81
Holborn ..	...	...		75
King's Cross	...	..	5	15
St. Pancras	...	...	5	15
Smithfield	...	...		79
Charing Cross	...	...	33	35
Moorgate ...	...	...		9
Elephant & Castle	...	...	33	35
Waterloo Station	...	...	33	35

1D.
2D.
3D.

Under Cover all the way by   (5d. Return)

LCC TRAMS

A London County Council advertisement for their tramway services to and from the Cattle Show at the Agricultural Hall. This was the event for which the venue was built, but nearly every other kind of display you could imagine took place here during the late Victorian and Edwardian periods.

The front page of the 1906 Cattle Show programme. Upper Street would have been thronged with visitors going to the show, and not just people in agriculture.

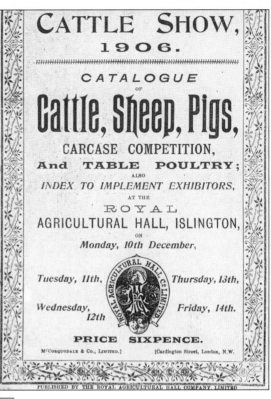

A pig gets a poke from a fashionable lady at a Victorian cattle show.

One of the more amazing events at the 'aggie' – a bull fight.

The early part of a six-day walking match. The author Peter Lovesey based a crime novel – *Wobble to Death*, around such an event at the Agricultural Hall.

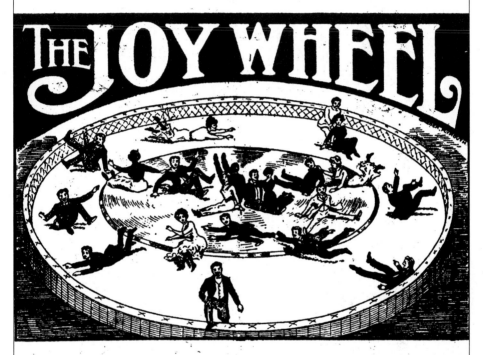

HELLO! IT HAS COME AT LAST.

WORLD'S FAIR

Agricultural Hall, Islington, N.

THE JOY WHEEL

If you do not like to go on the Joy Wheel yourself you can watch the others, and you will

ROAR WITH LAUGHTER !

It is the Funniest, the Jolliest, and the Best Show in the Fair. Everybody should see this before leaving the Fair.

DIRECT FROM CONEY ISLAND & BRUSSELS EXHIBITION.

THEOPHILUS CREBER, PRINTER, PLYMOUTH

The international World's Fair brought many exciting entertainments to Islington Green on a number of occasions.

This early Royal Tournament programme with its art nouveau decorations reminds us that this prestigious event was originally staged in Islington.

RASC riders at the 1928 Tournament.

FENCING.

BAYONET V. SWORD   (MOUNTED).

BAYONET V. SWORD (DISMOUNTED).

R. SIMKIN.

COMBATS.

Tournament combats – Victorian style. Many of the features of the show stayed the same over the years until its recent cessation.

Top left: A drawing of the old Collin's Music Hall and its proprietor Lew Lake, who still continued the tradition of the chairman by calling the patrons to order – typical of the nineteenth century Music Hall – in the early 1950s. The ebony gavel belonged to his great grandfather.

Top right: Comment in *The People* newspaper of 8 July 1900 on the week's programme of artists at Collin's. A theatrical journal of 1898 published this announcement: 'Next week, Collins Music Hall will be closed for a fortnight for renovations and the installation of electric light'. The old gas flares were relegated to the past.

Bottom left: Repairing bomb damage incurred during the Second World War. A surveyor's report on the auditorium (which could seat 1,000), shortly afterwards describes the survival qualities of the building: 'The condition of the structure is amazingly good. There is only one pillar in the lower part of the theatre, which means that the architect in 1897 must have anticipated the cantilever system now in use in modern cinemas'.

1958 Programme – the latter days of Collin's were filled with attempts to tempt customers away from new rival attractions such as television and pop music, using the lure of nude 'glamour girls'. During its long existence of over a hundred years, Collin's had seen appearances by nearly all the famous music hall 'stars' including Charlie Chaplin who of course became a world star in films, Gracie Fields, George Robey, Marie Lloyd, Harry Lauder and Bransby Williams.

A programme for The Grand Theatre, so named after a fire had burned down the former Philharmonic Music Hall on the same site and a new theatre constructed in its place in 1883. Some spectacular melodramas were presented here, including the re-opening piece *The New Babylon*. Fire claimed the theatre twice more in 1888 and 1900. Before the 1900 rebuild it saw some of Henry Irving's great roles, including Mathias in *The Bells*. Several other actor-managers brought their genius to this, 'One of the prettiest and best conducted theatres in London… ' The bottom picture shows the theatre advertising an early cinema or 'Biograph' moving pictures presentation.

THE GRAND THEATRE, ISLINGTON.
The Diamond Valley in the Pantomime, "Sinbad the Sailor," 1905-6.
[Copyright] [Photo Harry S. Lumsden

'The Grand' was often noted for the lavishness of its backdrops and scenery, as here with the Diamond Valley scene from *Sinbad the Sailor* in the winter season, 1905-06.

Even the goings-on outside the theatre were a spectacle for bystanders in 1910. This fine image shows a group of onlookers outside the Grand, now renamed the Islington Empire and a home for the variety theatre rather than the previously staged legitimate drama. From 1932 it became a cinema.

Here are 'Finlay Dunn's Dandies' whose agent produced this promotional postcard taken while they were putting on a performance at Southend. The address given is 1G Morgan Mansions, Highbury and they look as though their concert party services were in demand at theatres and bandstands around Britain, particularly at the many holiday resorts in the Edwardian days.

The Marlborough Theatre, Holloway.

One of Islington's prestigious entertainment venues – the Marlborough Theatre, Nags Head, Holloway in 1904. It was designed by the prolific Frank Matcham to hold an audience of 2,612. The opening saw a week of opera by the Carl Rosa Company. Many West End theatre companies played at this superior venue. From 1916 it became a variety theatre for a few years. Cinema took over from 1919-1957. The Polytechnic of North London was later built on the site.

The surprisingly exotic looking Holloway Empire designed by W.G.R. Sprague in 1899 is seen here, c. 1903. Famous music hall stars such as Harry Tate appeared here, but in 1912 it became a conventional theatre and later – by 1924 – a cinema. It closed in 1938 and lay derelict for many years. Later the site was developed as North Star House.

Canonbury Station, with its four platforms on the North London Railway, 1906. In the heyday of public transport in the late nineteenth and early twentieth centuries, few people owned cars. Yet all could easily get to and from local theatres and other attractions easily due to the great number of local stations and the frequency and late running of services.

DAYS WITH CELEBRITIES.   No. 473.
GRIMALDI.

Grimaldi, the famous clown and entertainer was much in vogue and as portrayed in this cameo, created a huge number of different characters. When this was published he had become a legend. Often playing at several theatres on the same evening – he arranged matters so that he could run between them and appear on the stage at just the right time. Sadler's Wells and Islington venues were the theatres that launched him during his lifetime (1779-1837) and helped him to bequeath his own name 'Joey' to the generations of clowns who followed him.

Five
Islingtonians

An unknown Islington lady captured in the rather severe style of the Victorian matron, by J.W. Gorsuch, an Upper Holloway studio. Islington has had many illustrious inhabitants, but it has often been the ordinary Islingtonians that have given the area its individuality, such as the flower ladies of Angel Market or the shopkeepers and dairymen of its main and side streets.

J.W. Gorsuch   48, JUNCTION RD
UPPER HOLLOWAY.

Charles Lamb, writer and essayist, lived for some time at Chapel Street and more notably at Duncan Terrace in Islington.

Colebrooke Cottage in the early 1930s. Originally, the New River flowed past the foot of its steps and when George Dyer – absent minded poet and Baptist minister – visited Lamb here he accidentally plunged into the water on leaving. This case of total immersion was lovingly recorded in *Amicus Redivivus* (A Friend Restored) one of the most well known pieces in *Essays of Elia*. A sadder tale is that of Lamb's sister Mary's descent into madness, when her brother led her over the fields to the south, on foot, to place her in the private insane asylum at Balmes House, Hoxton.

A distinguished resident of Highbury was Abraham Newland (1730-1807) who became chief cashier of the Bank of England in 1782. He lived at No. 38 Highbury Place, when he could tear himself away from the Bank where he often slept overnight. One of his clerks, Robert Aslett, embezzled money from the Bank and Newland was said to have died of a broken heart over this case.

The superior development of Highbury Place in the early nineteenth century. Its distinguished entrance gates have disappeared but the houses remain a source of architectural delight. Other famous residents have included Joseph Chamberlain, statesman and father of Neville, Prime Minister, at No. 25. The same house had previously seen frequent visits by John Wesley in 1770s, shortly after the houses were built. Walter Sickert also kept a studio and school of painting from 1927 to 1931 at No. 1.

SIR HUGH MYDDELTON, BART
THE PROJECTOR OF THE NEW RIVER AQUEDUCT.

Sir Hugh Myddelton was a great benefactor to Islington and London. He projected the New River scheme to bring a new source of water from springs in Hertfordshire to London during the reign of James I, even persuading the King to be a partner in the project. The 'river' was designed in the form of an aqueduct which conducted the water southward through Middlesex to a head pond next to Sadlers Wells. As the scheme matured, it produced some picturesque scenes such as that shown in the print, at Willow Bridge, Canonbury.

H. Winkles. del.t et sculp.t   VIEW, from near the Willow Bridge CANONBURY.

Alexander Aubert's name is connected with the raising of the Islington Volunteers during the days of fear about the possibility of a Napoleonic invasion of England. A volunteer in uniform is shown together with Aubert's house at Highbury. The man himself can be seen looking through a telescope on the roof.

View of HIGHBURY HOUSE the Seat of ALEX^R AUBERT ESQ^R.

The silhouette portrait is of the Marquess of Northampton in 1836. There have been connections between this family and Canonbury for several centuries. In 1570, Canonbury Tower which had been built in 1509 by Prior Bolton was acquired by John Spencer, a wealthy London merchant. He refused to allow his daughter Elizabeth to marry young Lord Compton – later the first Earl of Northampton – and shut her up in the tower. Lord Compton bribed servants to smuggle a rope into the building and Elizabeth was lowered down in a basket from her bedroom and the lovers eloped. Some time later Queen Elizabeth I commanded Spencer to attend a christening, and asked him to sponsor the baby. The ceremony over, the Queen asked the parents to come forth and Spencer, realising he had adopted his own grandson, was happily reconciled to his daughter.

What feats of strength were performed by Thomas Topham! It is believed that he was landlord of the Duke's Head, Islington. At the time he lifted three hogshead of water, 1,831 pounds at nearby Cold Bath Fields. This was on the 28 May 1741 to celebrate the taking of Porto Bello by Admiral Vernon. He performed the trial of strength in front of thousands of spectators and the Admiral himself. It was only one of many prodigious efforts of strength Topham achieved over the years.

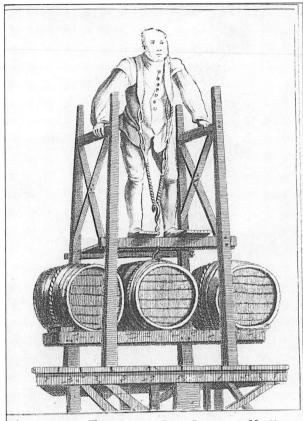

THOMAS TOPHAM, THE STRONG MAN.
Performing one of his astonishing feats of Strength in Spafields 28 of May 1741.

Thomas Cooke was a celebrated miser. He is seen here out walking with his housekeeper. Buried at St Mary's church, Islington, in 1811, Cooke had lived for many years in Winchester Place, Pentonville. A whole book about his strategems to avoid spending money was written by W. Chamberlaine, a surgeon, in 1814 – three years after Cooke's death at the age of eighty-five.

The children of St Mary's, Islington, Workhouse Guardians School making the most of

enjoying their sports day on 6 August 1913 at Dovercourt, Essex

Nell Smith, one of the group of younger women who were able to move into new areas of work after the First World War. So many men had been killed that there were gaps in the workforce. She found employment as a booking clerk on the underground railway (Metropolitan and Great Northern). She is standing by the old Highbury Fields exit from Highbury tube station.

Six
Streets, Broad and Narrow

St John Street, towards the Angel, *c.* 1906. The line of houses and shops with stucco fronts and balconies survived on both sides until the 1970s, when some of those on the left hand side were replaced by a modern tinted glass block. The single deck trams ran through to South London via a subway under the middle of the Aldwych, the Embankment and Westminster Bridge. They were later replaced by double decked trams and the Kingsway subway was doubled in height. The northern portal or entrance slope to this can still be seen.

Islington.   High Street.

The Angel corner with its horse buses and carts, still predominating at the very start of the twentieth century. An amazing multiplicity of business and entertainment facilities crammed the High Street.

Grosvenor Road on the borders of Highbury and Canonbury was a much quieter spot, *c.* 1911. The sender of this postcard has marked the house where he is staying. At this time with a population of over 330,000, there were few empty buildings in the borough.

St Mary's Road, Highbury in 1908. It contained large three storey houses with basements and a few attics. These were very typical Victorian homes, catering for the large and sometimes extended family units of those times. This pattern gradually broke down in the twentieth century, when more and more single tenants occupied small sections of such houses.

Highbury Grove.

Many of the houses standing in the tree lined avenues of 1908, as here in Highbury Grove, had substantial garden areas and outbuildings or stables. The large expanses of iron railings were to be taken down later during the Second World War by government decree in order to help the war effort. Thus the houses lost an element of privacy.

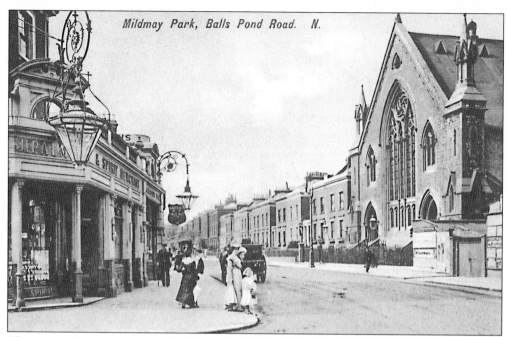

The corner where the bottom of Mildmay Park meets the Balls Pond Road, in 1907. The tavern on the left had very elaborate lamps typical of the era. The name Mildmay for street names in the area comes from the family with local landholdings dating back several centuries.

Another typical corner house with a tower dominated a section of Highbury Grove in the 1920s. The generous road width and the gated entrance to the private side road were distinguishing features of this part of the borough.

82

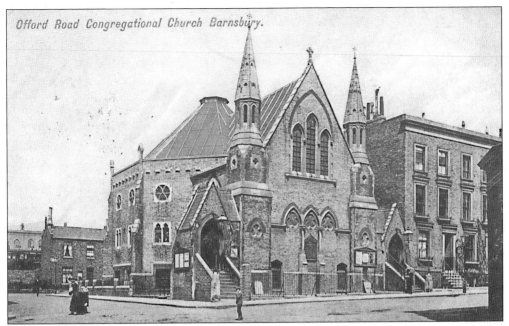

Offord Road Congregational Church Barnsbury.

Part of Offord Road's landscape, *c.* 1904. The Congregational Chapel was opened in April 1857 but closed in 1918, and merged with Arundel Square Chapel a couple of years later. In the 1980s the building was being used as a warehouse. On the far left beyond a grassy slope, a train can be seen in Barnsbury Station and beyond, a wing of Pentonville Prison.

Looking down Drayton Park, whose houses in this section are all on one side, railway land being to the left behind a wall, 1911. A station on the Great Northern and City tube railway had opened on 14 February 1904, putting the street on the map. But residents and shopkeepers must have been taken by surprise when in 1913 Arsenal Football Club relocated their grounds from Woolwich, South London to the next street. On match days henceforth, part of the crowd would wend its way via Drayton Park.

The Nags Head, Holloway area, looking from beyond Seven Sisters Road, *c.* 1921. Seven Sisters Road was begun in 1831 and opened for public use in 1833. The 'Seven Sisters' are trees at the Tottenham end where the road begins. The first trees, which were about 500 years old, began to decay in 1840.

So it became a fashion from then on for families of seven daughters to replant the trees (1852, 1888, 1955). Both the Holloway Road and Seven Sisters Road for some distance from the junction became great shopping areas in the late nineteenth and early twentieth centuries.

Highbury Terrace, built on the ridge above Highbury Fields, was definitely a superior place to reside at the time of this view in 1904 and for a hundred years before. Nos 1-16 had been built between 1789-1794. By 1829, there were sixteen houses of differing designs and by different architects. At No. 1 lived (Sir) Francis Ronalds (1788-1873) one of the pioneers – with Wheatstone – of the electric telegraph.

The imposing building in the middle of this picture at the junction of Camden and Parkhurst Roads was the Camden Road Athenaeum Literary and Scientific Institution, built in 1872 and demolished in 1956 – its replacement a petrol filling station. Behind the Athenaeum was the New Jerusalem Swedenborgian church. In the 1970s and the early 1980s this was the famous Islington Boys' Club.

Many passers-by have missed the interesting inscription above this mansion type building on the corner of Avenell Road and Aubert Park. It reads 'The Home for Confirmed Invalids', photographed, *c.* 1919.

Highbury New Park in 1905 could almost be called a boulevard with its wide carriageways lined with trees. The large dwellings are occasionally interrupted by a church, as seen here (St Augustine's, built 1870) and there was even a film studio. The road was too grand for bus routes. Charles Hambridge was the architect of the original italianate styled villas, the earliest being completed by December 1853.

A busy day outside the Nag's Head, Holloway at the beginning of the twentieth century. The prosperity of the neighbourhood at the time can be clearly seen. The pub is recorded in 1853 and the publicans for many years were the Wheeler family.

One of the most familiar views of Islington is that showing the apex of the tree-shaded 'Green', with Upper Street diverging to the left and Essex Road to the right, its horse bus on the return trip from Holborn. The Sir Hugh Myddelton statue adds a 'city' feel to the scene.

The very broad spaces of Petherton Road were described in the Annual Report of the Islington Vestry for 1881 as 'One of the noblest (streets) in this or any part of the Metropolis'. The New River formerly flowed in the open down the centre and was used by anglers. It was filled in to provide a processional route.

Highbury Corner with the old Cock Tavern on the right. A horse tram of the era (1904) is on its way from Highgate to Moorgate in the City. The tall and narrow frontages of the former houses of Upper Street are crammed with offices and shops as well as private dwellings.

At the heart of things – Upper Street by the Star and Garter in the 1920s. Motoring is becoming popular with the more well-to-do, and there is a line up of cars along the stepped and raised section of the pavement. On the pavement a sign points to a garage on the opposite side of the road behind the photographer. The sheer variety of individual traders is what takes the

eye. In this small section of street we have costumiers, fancy linen-drapers, blind makers, hatters and glovers (these important accessories worn by many at the time) also sellers of dressing cases, jewellery, beads, clocks, earthenware, brushes and ironmongery as well as furriers and several other trades.

A house in Liverpool Road displayed many signs of life in the past. The chimneys still very much in use, point to the coal fire heating inside. The delicate iron balconies indicate the origin of the houses in a more gracious era. The railings in front protect the basements, where perhaps the cook and other servants dwelt. The two doors have knockers rather than bells and a brass tradesman's plate announces the service provided to the community. Thousands of these were once fixed to the fronts of houses providing a directory before the advent of 'Yellow Pages'.

Seven
A Place of Learning

Award presentation time for the Islington Drill Brigade, an organization that appears on the evidence to have been run mainly for girls. The nearest to this today might be the majorettes, youth marching bands and cheerleaders.

At the beginning of the century the modern role models, pop stars, footballers and disc jockeys were unheard of but there was a cult of honouring the country's military and naval leaders, and the pioneers who helped to create and maintain our world wide empire were also highly thought of. As England was a highly jingoistic nation at the time, the leadership idea was much in vogue.

Captain Baker of the IDB as it was familiarly known, is here shown as a fine military looking figure of a man, though what his qualifications were exactly, are not known – being able to command respect among other adults at the time being enough.

A smart turnout of the brigade youngsters with Capt. Baker in charge.

Mr J. Pearce was vice-president of an obviously well-structured organization. His photograph shows him in his role of elder statesman to the brigade.

A group of brigade members are seen in their nattily designed uniforms which were part of the organization's attractions. There is quite a suggestion of naval uniform – the Royal Navy being at the height of popularity at the beginning of the twentieth century – every child knew about Nelson and other heroic naval actions. A few boys appear in the picture, two of them holding the banner.

Five selected girl leaders on parade.

A group apparently hoping to join the brigade are greeted on the steps of the school hall.

The Tollington Park Central School athletes with their trophies, 1922-23.

Pupils are out of school at the Cumberland Street and St Clements Schools, Barnsbury. Any pupil with at least half an old penny to spend would be off to the tuck shop.

This appears to be an Empire Day Parade at a Holloway school, *c.* 1908. Empire Day was often celebrated with great ceremony of flags and speeches. Sometimes, the pupils dressed up in

costumes from every part of the British Empire – 'on which the sun never sets'.

For nearly 400 years from 1613, the school founded by Dame Alice Owen was located off St John Street near the Angel. Dame Alice had survived a near miss by an arrow from a bowman practising on the butts in the fields between the City and Islington, not far away. After outlasting three husbands, she fulfilled a promise made after her miraculous escape by founding almshouses and a school. This statue stood in the entrance hall at Islington – executed by Frampton it was one of the finest productions of the nineteenth century English School of Sculpture.

The Owen's Almshouses in St John Street in the early nineteenth century. The school occupied a wing on the right. The school retained the gates shown in front of the almshouses up until the end of its Islington existence. Closure came in 1976, after a new school opened in Potters Bar.

OWEN'S SCHOOL

TRUSTEES :
THE WORSHIPFUL COMPANY OF BREWERS

Report for the Half-year ending _February_ 19 _53_.

Name _B D Evans_ Age _15. 9_ Form _V. A._

Place in Form | Term | Exam. | Final

Number of Boys _28_ Average Age _15. 9_

SUBJECT	EXAMINATIONS Per-centage Marks	EXAMINATIONS Place in Form or Set	REMARKS
RELIGIOUS KNOWLEDGE			
ENGLISH LANG.	67	10	A thoughtful & hard worker. He should do well. _RQU._
ENGLISH LIT.	53	6	
MATHEMATICS ALG. 50 GEOM 13 ARITH 47	37	SET II 8/23	These results are rather disappointing as he has worked extremely well throʼout the year. _S.P.W_
HISTORY	54	5	He always works well and thoroughly. He is somewhat slow to learn examination tactics, when he does so he will do better. _S.G.S._
GEOGRAPHY			
LATIN	65	8	Good work and progress. _G.A.H._
FRENCH	63	14	Getting on satisfactorily. _H.H._
GERMAN	59	6/13	Should do quite well if he continues to work hard. _B.B_
SCIENCE			

ATTENDANCE : ABSENT _1_ DAYS, AND LATE _0_ TIMES. FIRST DAY OF NEXT TERM _28th April._

CONDUCT : DETENTION _0_ AND CONDUCT CLASS _0_ TIMES. LAST DAY OF NEXT TERM _29th July._

Very promising, but, as above, he must attend to the Mathematics. _H. Harduck_ FORM MASTER.

Good. He must however note every comment. _W.L. Garstang_ HEADMASTER.

A typical school report from of the early 1950s. When Elizabeth acceded to the throne on the death of her father George VI in 1952, the pupils were assembled in the school hall and told that they were the 'New Elizabethans' entering a new modern era of progress. The school was in 'The Headmasters Conference,' an elite group of Grammar and Public Schools. The blazer badge at top right incorporates the arrows symbolising Alice Owen's providential escape as a girl, and the Arms of the Brewer's Company of the City of London. Other special school badges, for instance for sport and other awards, displayed her family badge of the pomegranate.

101

Holloway College at No. 30 Hartham Road was founded in 1864. The pupils of an Edwardian intake stand on the steps of the rather attractive building set in its own gardens.

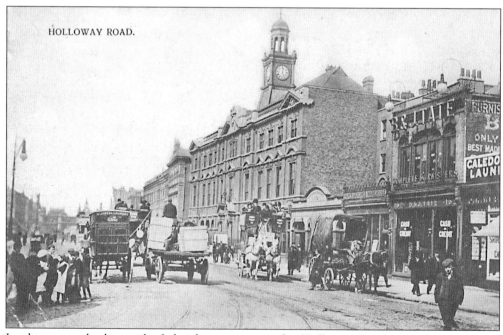

In the centre background of this busy scene in the Holloway Road around 1904 is the impressive frontage of the famous Northern Polytechnic, a bastion of further education in the twentieth century. The building was designed by Charles Bell and opened in 1896 on the site of Osnaburgh Cottages, but was extensively added to by A.W. Cooksey shortly after, in 1902.

Clarks College was started in this house in Southgate Road, Islington by a young War Office civil servant amazingly in his off duty hours in the evening, in 1880. From these small beginnings a chain of Clark's Colleges spread across England and became much sought after as a source of progressive commercial education.

The Holloway branch of Clark's in 1905 in its large corner house. Details of its courses are posted on the notice boards above the perimeter wall. The hansom cabs could have graced a Sherlock Holmes story.

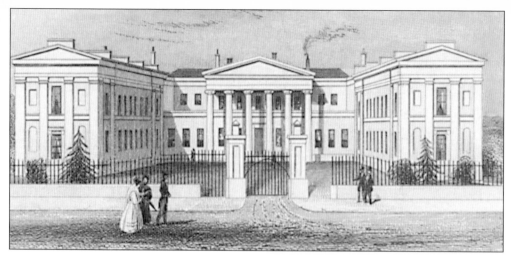

An early nineteenth-century print of Highbury College and two later photographs, showing it in its latter days as St John's Hall. It was a theological college which moved from Mile End to Highbury in 1826. In 1913, its grounds were sold to become the Arsenal Football Club stadium.

Eight
Made in Britain

Islington's role as an important centre for shopping and entertainment has been mentioned. Another side of its diverse activity was as an area with a large number of industrial and engineering works, and firms involved with the distribution of such products.

Islington's Royal Agricultural Hall became a centre for trade exhibitions of all kinds. A view of an early motor show at this venue displayed motor cars produced in Britain and many other countries. But Islington's own products came from a wide range of trades, from bed manufacture to high class building work (cathedrals, churches and public buildings).

Early factories in the fields. There were two floor cloth manufacturers operating in the early nineteenth century. The top print shows the scene, close to Copenhagen House, near to the new Chalk (later Caledonian) Road in a rural situation. At the bottom is Samuel Ridley's works in the Lower (later Essex) Road. This building survived into the twentieth century under various guises, particularly Probyn's bottling works.

The Regent's Canal in the early nineteenth century, viewed from near Thornhill Bridge towards the tunnel where it passes under the Islington ridge (Gisla's Dune from which Islington gets its name). The proximity of the canal benefited and encouraged industrial and other concerns to locate nearby. The other side of the tunnel took the canal to the City Basin, conveniently near many City activities.

A Great Northern Railway steam train approaches the now long closed Holloway and Caledonian Road station, north of King's Cross, which was once served by a stopping service appropriate for this densely populated area. Holloway Road underground station took over from the mainline service. The importance of the railways as a carrier of both raw and finished materials in the nineteenth and earlier twentieth century cannot be underestimated.

TROTMAN & CO.'S

Illustrated Catalogue of

Baby Carriages,
Baby Chairs,
Mail Carts,
etc.

TERMS: CASH,
and Cash Only.

High-class Finish
Handsome Designs
Coach-built Bodies
Newest Patterns

West End Style
Lasting Wear
Latest Inventions
Lowest Price

TROTMAN'S is the Oldest
Carriage Firm in London.

TERMS: CASH,
and Cash Only.

Only Address: **196, HOLLOWAY ROAD, N., 196**

Between Highbury, N. L. R., and Holloway, G. N. R., and close to and same side as Northern Polytechnic.

The "COSY" CHAIR.

The greatest triumph in Baby Chairs. Convertible to 7 positions, viz.:— High Chair, Low Chair, go cart and rocker, reclining, bed position, and reversible table. N.B.—The reclining and bed position can be used in combination with any of the other five positions.

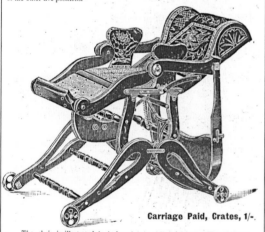

Carriage Paid, Crates, 1/-.

The chair is illustrated in bed and low chair positions. The ordinary positions of chair are same as those as "Baby's Friend," illustrated in this catalogue. The "Cosy" Chair is most useful, very handsome, and thoroughly reliable, and is upholstered in **Velvet, Plush, or Morocco,** and made in three varieties:

A. UPHOLSTERED BACK AND RAIL TOP 27/6
B. UPHOLSTERED BACK, SIDES, AND ROLL TOP ... 29/6
C. UPHOLSTERED BACK, SIDES, AND CRADLE HEAD-GUARDS,
   AS ILLUSTRATED 32/6
A., B., C., upholstered in Morocco, **2/6** extra; Velvet Cushions, **2/6** extra.

To Mothers.—Please notice that if baby should fall asleep whilst sitting up, a slight movement of chair converts it into a comfortable bed without disturbing or waking the child. No mother or nurse would be without this Baby Chair if they only knew its great advantages. It is unique and can be recom-

Trotman's – one of Islington's home industries. The cover of a turn-of-the-century catalogue is shown. As well as prams, the firm produced other items such as the baby chair (left) – a strange and ungainly item to modern eyes, but remember, this was before the days of plastic.

108

An old billhead from Jules Lang and Son – glass manufacturers and 'general merchant shippers'. Their office in Charlton Place was once a quiet backwater.

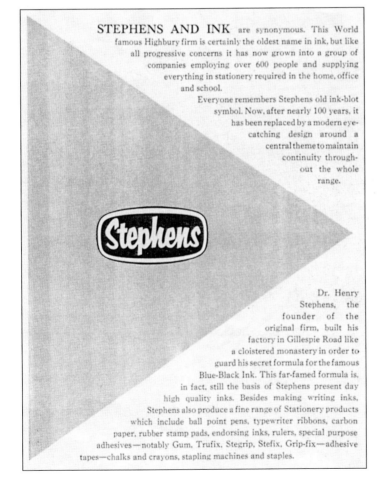

STEPHENS AND INK are synonymous. This World famous Highbury firm is certainly the oldest name in ink, but like all progressive concerns it has now grown into a group of companies employing over 600 people and supplying everything in stationery required in the home, office and school.

Everyone remembers Stephens old ink-blot symbol. Now, after nearly 100 years, it has been replaced by a modern eye-catching design around a central theme to maintain continuity throughout the whole range.

Dr. Henry Stephens, the founder of the original firm, built his factory in Gillespie Road like a cloistered monastery in order to guard his secret formula for the famous Blue-Black Ink. This far-famed formula is, in fact, still the basis of Stephens present day high quality inks. Besides making writing inks, Stephens also produce a fine range of Stationery products which include ball point pens, typewriter ribbons, carbon paper, rubber stamp pads, endorsing inks, rulers, special purpose adhesives—notably Gum, Trufix, Stegrip, Stefix, Grip-fix—adhesive tapes—chalks and crayons, stapling machines and staples.

This ingenious advertisement gives a potted history of Stephen's Ink's Islington origins.

109

Knowlman Brothers of Upper Holloway line up their transport fleet. The firm was a

bedding specialist.

WE HAVE HELPED over 50,000

DANCE ORGANISERS, CLUB SECRETARIES, HOTELIERS, etc., etc., MAKE A GREATER SUCCESS OF THEIR JOB BY VIRTUE OF OUR VAST EXPERIENCE IN THE CARNIVAL TRADE AND OUR EXTENSIVE VARIETY OF . . .

FANCY HATS
TRUMPETS
BLOWOUTS
STREAMERS
BALLOONS
MASKS, WIGS
NOSES, FANS
PARTY BOXES
TRICKS, JOKES
DOYLEYS, TOYS
JELLY CASES
SERVIETTES
XMAS CRACKERS
MUSICAL TOYS
MOUSTACHES
BADGES
CLOAKROOM AND RAFFLE TICKETS
BALLROOM POLISH
FLAGS, RATTLES
CREPE PAPER
DECORATIONS

We shall be pleased to send a Catalogue on request. Write to Dept "G"

BECKS BRITISH CARNIVAL NOVELTIES
139 UPPER STREET, LONDON, N.1 Tel. CANonbury 2045 (2 lines)

Beck's British Carnival Novelties used this fun advertisement to publicise their activities in the 1960s.

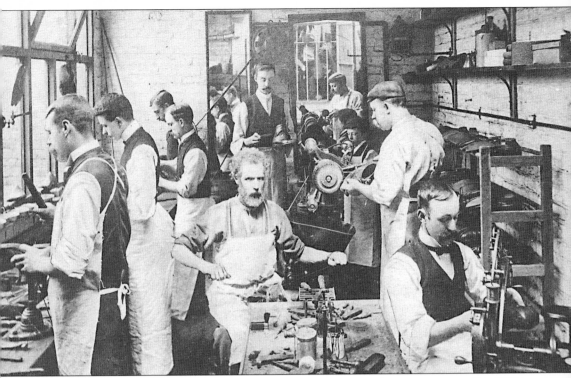

This is Mulholland's workshop, Nos 53-55 Seven Sisters Road, at the beginning of the twentieth century. The workshop complex employed electricity to repair and manufacture boots – the standard footwear of the time for both work and everyday use among ordinary people.

Trotman's Mangles and Rubber Wringers,

☞ FOR CASH. ☜

One Quality only:

THE BEST!

One Price only:

THE LOWEST!

Every- Machine is Warranted!

RUBBER WRINGERS.		MANGLES and WRINGERS.	
Best Rubber only, vulcanised on shafts, wood or galvanised frame.		18-in., Stout Rollers ...	**32.6**
		20-in. „ ...	**37/6**
10-in., **10/6**	11-in., **12/6**	22-in. „ ...	**39/6**
12-in., **14/6**	14-in., **17/6**	24-in. „ ...	**42/-**

The above are WARRANTED; we supply a cheaper and good line, but not warranted, from 7/6 each.

Carriage Paid in London. Outside London, Mangles, 2/6 ; Rubber Wringers, 1/-

Another line of Trotman's products were these ironmongery items. Before the days of washing machines every home possessed mangles and wringers.

It was fitting that a strategically placed borough such as Islington with its concentration of business and industry should be the home of a large Post Office complex, in Manor Gardens, Upper Holloway, which among other things housed the Money Order department.

Nine
The Northern Heights

A scene of chaos at Highgate Archway, at the foot of the steep incline of West Hill down which the electric tram on the left has run away due to brake failure.

A closer view of the Archway Tavern, 1904. The photograph clearly shows the importance of the horse at this date – on the far left a delivery van, a milk cart, the two horse trams,

and the two horse buses to the right. In such a crowded place horses instinctively moved to avoid collisions and were more manoeuvrable than early motor buses.

The building of the bypass route through the Archway led to a toll bar and gate being erected at the foot of the hill, *c.* 1813. The toll was 4 old pence a horse, and one old penny for foot passengers. This was still collected up until 1876.

The old narrow highway through John Nash's Archway, built of stone but flanked by brickwork. Its foundation stone was laid on 31 October 1812 and it stood till 1898/99. There was also a pedestrian way through the arch, which cannot be seen in this illustration.

These two pictures show the benefits of widening the arch – the easy flow of traffic and two good pavements on either side with plenty of light. The new design, shown here, was the work of Sir Alexander Binnie and stretches 59.2ft from road level to road level. The new bridge was opened by Princess Louise, Duchess of Argyll.

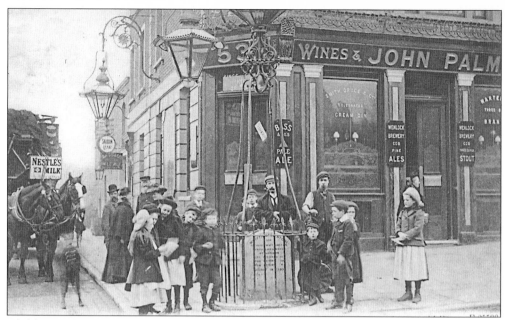

Children and a few adults gather round the Whittington Stone on Highgate Hill. The site was between Brunswick (now MacDonald) and Salisbury Roads. In medieval times there was a lepers' field of the Chapel of St Anthony in this area (recorded in the fifteenth century). The stone was once a pyramid with a cross on top where food or alms were left for the lepers. The scene outside the pub in 1905 includes some village gossip going on next to the horse bus whose driver has alighted.

A close up of the stone in the late 1940s. An officious parish post holder of 1795 broke up the medieval stone. After this two replacements followed, the most recent in 1821. A repair was made in 1935, and in 1950 it was reset with a new surround of railings. Owing to road improvements and vandalism the stone was moved to near the corner of Magdala Avenue. In 1964 Donald Bissett, an actor and children's author, commissioned the figure of a cat to be set on the top of the stone.

St Joseph's church and retreat. A striking group of buildings forming a well known landmark on Highgate Hill as seen in the 1920s, known affectionately to generations of Islingtonians as 'Holy Joe's'. The retreat was founded in 1858 by Father Ignatius Paoli (1818-85). In 1888, the corner stone of the new St Joseph's was laid. The architect, A. Vicars, designed a 107ft high dome. Adjoining is the monastery of the Passionist Fathers, opened in 1876. St Joseph's church was consecrated in 1932 – there are also schools and a parish hall.

OLD COTTAGES,

Although most of the old cottages like those above have disappeared, there is still an old world appeal about the middle and upper parts of Highgate Hill. The subtle curves of the view below together with the remaining characterful structures set on the steep slopes impart a uniqueness to the vicinity. The electric trams are gone in favour of diesel buses but they would certainly have been a tourist attraction today.

Highgate Hill

122

A Victorian house in Tufnell Park, No. 69
Brecknock Road in October 1912. The road
was developed in the second half of the
nineteenth century.

Southcote Road in 1906. This Tufnell Park street, built in 1884, was at this point in time
completely traffic free so that youngsters could use the middle of the road for games.

Junction Road in the 1920s – another atmospheric scene showing the importance of local shops before widespread car ownership. The shops along the nearest parade certainly catered for wide ranging needs. With car congestion reaching new heights in the twenty-first century, there is a

hint of a return to these old ideas. In the parade at least one shop spills out onto the pavement
– almost certainly a greengrocer's.

At the north east corner of the borough is Crouch Hill railway station with its simple booking hall and entrance built over the cutting. In 1903, the station area was a centre of activity with a significant group of neighbourhood shops with their line of dedicated lamps outside – a sight not encountered today.

This quaint section of Hornsey Lane at the top end of the borough retains its high pavement as a protection for pedestrians. The interesting house with an overhanging gable and the bollards on the right create a charming scene, along with the Edwardian passers-by.

The exterior of the unusual Aged Pilgrims Friend Society housing project, Hornsey Rise, has a welcoming aspect in the picture above. Below we see a room in the excellent and homely accommodation provided by the charity, furnished with the treasures of the residents.

THE COTTAGE,
HORNSEY LANE, 1880.

W. WEST.
No 29.

Loretto House and the Cottage, Hornsey Lane in 1880. In the drive towards modern comfort and uniformity, so many interesting corners of Islington have been trampled underfoot. It is now necessary to look closely to find those that are left.